Sea Change

Sea

poems by

Christopher Howell

illustrations by

Carol Jablonsky

L'Epervier Press

Change

KNIGHT-CAPRON LIBRARY
LYNCHBURG COLLEGE
LYNCHBURG, VIRGINIA 24501

ACKNOWLEDGMENTS

Some of the poems in this volume first appeared in the following periodicals: *The Antioch Review, The Carleton Miscellany, Chicago Review, The Iowa Review, Cutbank, Groundwater Review, Happiness Holding Tank, Ironwood, The Massachusetts Review, The Minnesota Review, The Northwest Review, The Penny Dreadful, Memphis State Review, Mississippi Mud, Poetry Northwest, Portland Review, Three Sisters,* and *Umbral.*

"The Wu General Writes from Far Away" appeared in *Pushcart III: The Best of the Small Presses* (The Pushcart Press, Yonkers, N.Y., 1978). It also appeared in *Rain in the Forest, Light in the Trees* (Owl Creek Press, Missoula, Mt., 1983).

"Paid in Full" appeared in *The Umbral Anthology of Science Fiction Poetry* (Umbral Press, Denver, Colo., 1982).

A few of the poems also appeared in the following limited edition volumes:
    The Crime of Luck, Panache Books, 1976
    The Bear in the Mirror, Raincrow Press, 1977
    Red Alders in an Island Dream, Trask House Books, 1980

The publication of this book was made possible in part by the King County Art Commission's Small Press Publication Award.

The author wishes to thank the National Endowment for the Arts for the Creative Writing Fellowship which helped support him while these poems were being written. Special thanks also to David Luckert for his generous and sensitive editorial suggestions, and to Carol Jablonsky for her evocative and delightful images.

Poems copyright 1985 by Christopher Howell
Illustrations copyright 1985 by Carol Jablonsky

Howell, Christopher.
    Sea change.

    I. Title.
PS3558.0897S4   1985   811'.54   84-26112
ISBN 0-934332-41-X pbk
ISBN 0-934332-43-6

Book design by Bridget Culligan, Seattle, WA

L'EPERVIER PRESS

for Sweetgum

CONTENTS

I
In Conflict with His Shadow

3   THE MAN WHO HOPED
4   PROPHETIQUE
5   THE WU GENERAL WRITES FROM FAR AWAY
7   MUSIC FROM A CUP OF FRUIT
8   THE SEARCH FOR STEPHEN SKJEI
11 THE VOYAGE
12 AVIARY: SONNET IN RETURN ORBIT
13 RAMON'S LETTER
14 DREAM FOR THE CAPE OF GOOD HOPE
15 TREASON THE COMFORTER
16 ANGEL IN THE TORN RED COAT
18 PAID IN FULL
19 ENOUGH
20 SEASCAPE

II
Sea Change

25 BEYOND THE DREAM HATCH
26 THE DREAMS OF CELLOS
27 CINNAMON IS THE SECRET
28 THE PITCHER'S PRIDE
29 CHANCE
30 SPIRIT HOVERING ABOVE THE BOX
31 LIBERTY & TEN YEARS OF RETURN
34 GREETING THE GHOSTLY ROSE
35 IN FOUR PARTS
36 LIGHT, SUDDEN, BREAKS IN SHAFTS FROM HER
37 NOTES
38 TWO FOR JAMES WRIGHT
40 A REMINDER TO THE CURRENT PRESIDENT
42 THE TELL-TALE ANGEL
43 ON THE LAREDO LINE
44 THE DREAMER'S FUTURE
45 ABOARD THE DAN JUAN FERRY

III
Sotto Voce

49 THREE DEATHS AND ANOTHER START
50 ONE VISION
51 FIRST SNOW
52 IN GREY WATER: THE DAY
56 OR LAUGH
57 FLIGHTS THE WIRE BIRD WATCHES
58 AT THE EQUINOX
60 THE DEATH OF GIOVINE
61 GESTURE TO THE CAGED CRICKET
62 KEEPING WATCH UNDER A LAMP POST . . .
64 WHAT WAS A THIN WIRE

I
IN CONFLICT
WITH HIS SHADOW

And the beasts of the desert awaited the coming of night on the other side of the cliffs. You could see the light through the wings of the soaring birds. In autumn the storks came from those faraway lands, they said, where I am now, and where I have never seen any.

Michel Butor
Passage de Milan

THE MAN WHO HOPED

He formed his rose
against a stone
and spoke to the god.
The god said paint it
the color a stone weaves
at dawn, paint it
rose. But it was
not that sort of day.
He took willows from a box
in his soul. They were green
like snow is green, like blind men
in a spring wind.
What could he hope for,
pearls? He spoke to the god.
And the god said yes
hope for pearls.

PROPHETIQUE

The moon wishes against a pearl disguise of cloud.
October. No one astonished
except the one goose flying north with fanatical certainty

While all the others fly south from winter's helmsman
unfurling his jolly roger in the pines.
How many tickets clasped in his too-white teeth?

What would you give to know? Their color
is orange, like air at the edge of a season.
Their direction is a displaced femur

upon which is written, "How many legs will you need
in the next world?" Go on flying, the answer and the urge
to speak it not in you and not in the things you love.

THE WU GENERAL WRITES FROM FAR AWAY

My dear friend
       It is snowing
in the house of my body, and beyond tarnishing
childhood song, below the red
black earth our grandfathers loved.
       What shall I say of this Summer
in which it is snowing
so often? I have no voice to describe
the delicacy of grasses, the scarlet horns
of new birds crying *feed feed*.
Every swayed limb stops the world
freshly. Every doe
browsing in sunlight beyond the meadow of tents
is a woman
releasing her braid on plain white silks.
       But it is going, it is all
going again through glass lips
of the hour. Soon cold will step from hiding;
the bears stagger comically to sleep; poor
beggars die out the crime of luck. Even now
courtesans lean to practiced grace
alone, shamed
as brushes draw youth on.
       Where shall we find hope
that cruelty is a passing accident, balance
the true gauge?
       I long to speak again kindly
with the thin dead
blossoms
who followed me here. I want to caress
the rose of peace before it empties; to abandon
storms over the ancestors of bodiless order.
       Tell me you have found it, the drowned
key, the footprint waking peacocks
at the last minute
which stops. You who followed the absent fortune

of pilgrims, come back to your friend
rooted here, sealed
in harm's garden of jars. Tell all
before snow retakes the road
to feeling,
this foreign ground.

MUSIC FROM A CUP OF FRUIT

Mozart enters and circles the room.
Where is the cup of fruit, gift
from Hapsburgs in a difficult time?
The pears and berries of wax
loose their pale lights somewhere.
Where? Why, Wolfgang wonders, does
such beauty turn its face?

Drawing the satin sashes wide
and peering over rooftiles
to the street, he drinks the mystery
of panic. Things get lost, Herr Mozart,
things die out and are maimed
by terrible struggle or by others
whose losses made them cruel.

Sitting against the wall, he thinks
he must weep. But he doesn't weep.
He lifts his arms into an amazement
of harmony and two-four desire,
solid, humming like blood. And then
he begins to write and we cannot reach him,
cry out as we will that he has left us,
that his loss was ours, that
it was all we had.

THE SEARCH FOR STEPHEN SKJEI

I

I do not know the weight
of sorrow driving you
into the grey grass of twilight
or some other faded place.
That was long ago, and anyway
all little bastard angels hide
their eyes when sun goes down.
We never saw a thing. The future
just took you, shying off
wounded into the marshes
south of Spanaway.
Some say it was a woman
or a father, lost clarinet of self, that pulled your pin.
It may have been the drugs.
You went
flying the bicycle of low sun
striking a lake, and left us
calling "Stephen" into the darkening
calendar. What treasures
did you take
that we wonder after you
across a cruel decade of snows
and apple blossoms?
Birds cough in the dirty pines
like so many sickened clocks.
We know you'll not be back
repaired and steady in the air
breathing us like reeds.

II

I can't speak
for Bohm, Gaylord and the rest;
but I am dying
of the things I loved
to break. That one I married once,
for instance, sticks in my rib
of care; wooden stake
that missed the heart.
And those I have betrayed, God
help my hands paint every night
the fresh ruby lists of face.
No help. Also
no rose clings to any space
on which I fix a roof. Fifteen cities
stagger in my spine, that starved road
bearing north toward your last known
habitation, the mountain
of lost shoes.

III

Gone for good. A rocking chair
comforts wind
on a grey front porch. Look
how willows toss their fountainous green
in the 12 year echo of your step.
We miss you
as we miss the gods
thrown down by great denial
and despair. Gone forever
not for good, not for any island
in the calm burn of our mutilated star
the past. Gone
like life goes, casting
you this final useless vote:
Stephan, out in mist and smoke,
take care
of longing, it is all
you keep.

THE VOYAGE

An obsidian boat vibrates
in the heart of a cloud
above Martinique. The crew,
in chains, moves with blue insistence
toward the idea of water.
The sky is solid waves
of rock. Wind ignites the only map.
Now and then something alive
is thrown overboard. "No one
asked you to come along,"
the Captain, horrible gob of dissolutions,
says, pouring another glass
of fire. "Well, you're in for it
if you think this is bad!" Claws
come out of the deck
and deal with the complainers.
It is a huge enterprise, by all accounts,
revolutionary. They are going to discover
the Islands of Commerce, those bland
and equitable kingdoms
where success is breathable, not a lie
at all. The ship yaws, taking on lava
and screams. "Oh they don't
make a bloody crew like they used,"
the Captain observes, boiling hideously.
The boat, *Lucky Forever,* steams
into a treatise on late 20th century
starvation, where it capsizes. The Captain,
secretly sure all along that the voyage
has been madness, says, "Christ!
we should have stayed in Hell."

AVIARY: SONNET IN RETURN ORBIT

By the canal
among ducks and teal and the watchful
loons, your right breast with its rose
insists we will embrace,
walk on, embrace
again. The *softness*
of the intersliding leaves and light!
You cock your head at terns
gracing the long radium kiss
of water, its back
bent through a hall of trees
in which the blue canaries sing
You've lost her and she's lost you
and this is our dream get out.

RAMON'S LETTER

I broke the stone
I did not mean to break
the nightingale
caged preciously in the digress
moment of today's mail. Ramon,
this year was wet; last year cloudless
and dry — the inland gulls became beige
drifts of dust. I continue in my faith
that lilacs will sweeten me
if I eat enough of them.
Stubble and wind and a headlight
drunkeness keep me
a little sad. Also, I thicken, like a tree,
roots bursting into the cistern
on a nondescript afternoon in March.
You write no letters, but I get news
of you; how you sit
piquant, tilted back with a beer
and a garnet arrow which is called
virgin. Feed it the broken nightingale,
why don't you, the shards of rock.
Be sure the smokey blood left over
makes someone weep for that face
of yours, catching the brick
Auld Lange Syne of love
delivered for a fee.

DREAM FOR THE CAPE OF GOOD HOPE

The light on the jailer's face
is corpse-light. It rhymes
from the cages that clang
in bellies; from memories sliding
to the ends of the prisoners' hair.
It isn't morning by the rack
and torture baths. Jailer:
his voice is a tower to count
on your elbows one two
one two, in secret. Bolt and bar:
his voice is the falcon sketching
ghost towns of rabbit, a soul
full of rats. Come out.
It will never be morning
at the rented graves.
Come out like wine
turned water in shallow
deployments of the key
statutes. Come out
conscripted, *breeders*. The jailer's
throat is pale chain, willow root
groping, exposed to sky
and rock falling
falling like an axe from the dark
keep.

TREASON THE COMFORTER

Wheelhouse   *Crippling*   *Day-of-rest*
From tall grass three different bird song: the name plates
of angels; one burning.

Stiletto   *Sea Cow*   *Whip*
No money is release from pain, no tide is bloodless.
Did you think yourself better than others?

Mad   *Dimness*   *Hold me*
The inner paneling of certain stars: momentary,
except for the life-long wind of no ones.

Judas   *Woodheart*   *What could I do*
All wisdom is snow, likewise folly: like you, brother,
dead by rope and an odd silver impulse hammered out
in advance.

ANGEL IN THE TORN RED COAT

Where once a countess danced
and made her lover dance
with a sudden blade,
the angel in a torn red coat
shakes his tambourine, shuffles
and cuts his deck
and deals:

One King for the beanflower,
sweetest garden fool.
Queen for the unmourned innocently
dead, for the ditch
of power. *Jack* for judgment
and sentence.
Jack for what endures the cold
claws of avarice and weather.
Ace that pays whatever bell
will wake the bearer.
Ten and *Nine* for the leaves
that fall in tens and nines.
Two for the carriage windows
ghost and yellow
on ghostly snow. *Seven*
for the bloodied lover left
by the Helsinki road; no luck,
he had it coming.

Tambourine like a silvered heart
beside him, the angel contemplates
his cards on icy ground, touching
their names, again, holding in
his dingy feathers under the bright
velvet. On his back, in large blue,
"We're Open." Such is death
and life, he would say: always

by a road somewhere in some kind
of light. Always wondering what
had got into the Countess or the State
or circumstance. Always stabbing wings
through your brand new coat.

PAID IN FULL

A man opens his mouth to spit or speak rapidly.
Thousands of erasers tumble out.
They are the silence keeping ahead of him, the lack
of a future, the history he will not look back on
that will not look back on him.
                                           The erasers gather
lovingly around him, erasing first the mouth
then the nose, ears, and the rest of the face.
Leaving the eyes, tragic and wide, in a clear space
above the body.

Through the eyes the man watches
all the dear labor of him
erased, beginning with carefully chosen cigars
and personal accoutrements.
                                        The rug and walls
go quickly. The wife takes a long slow sob of hours.
The arsenic blue floating eyes widen and fill with blood.
The man's body disappears in a frenzy
                                                of pink shavings. Now
only the terrible eyes plead
                         in a windy field.

The man who is not
sees that all things are without him.
He sees the beauty of before he was,
                                         or after.
He sees the erasers writing on the frosted glass
of Heaven: *All speech and all longing*
to speak erases the self, to some degree.
Now you are paid in full.

ENOUGH

I give you this one road
dusty with circling gnats, a figure
moving south in the heat.
Do you like it
enough? I give you also a sandy taste,
a blue eye blacked by some misstep
in Laredo when the liquor burned
its slow down-shift
                    behind the ruined jail.
Not enough? Take the figure (man) then
wholly, the story he walks in like a trail
of printed shoes.
Take his sons and the women who threw him out
hissing *bastard!* Take all the loading dock jobs
and night escapes to Umatilla and Brush.
Let his face shine out in your rear-view
as you punish the air
                    of the future dissolving
in your lifted hair. Wish him dead
or wish him a paper swan
bowing to the moon on water.
Still he walks, faded green light
leaking from a satchel.
He is by you in bed with that one twisted
beauty you cannot forget. His hand and hers
groan together
                down the wet highway
of your thrusting spine. It matters, the story
that he is not dead now
or tomorrow — in spite of whatever you wish.
That he lifts
one foot and sets it down in dust
you remember (the throttle!) as it rushes
over you like wind crying *enough.*
enough for you.

SEASCAPE

*Out on the Pacific, in that green
air studded with sharks,
a veil is blowing over the ghost ships
of Miguel Ortiz. What gold or love
or language in them, the dolphins know.*

*

On your raft, be quiet
about the lack of food and the way
current guides your death
with huge paws. If you could catch
a dolphin, it would only be a singer,
dancer in the heavy wind
like you. If you could call out like an unmuzzled star
to the great whale within you dreaming
of another age, you would lie to him
always. This is fate, voice awash in the chest
wound of the sea. Listen
at your peril, but listen if you can.
Lost is just a word; like *cloud*,
like *homeward* and *chain*. It isn't yours,
drifting planet, anymore. Nothing itself
swims past the reefed dictionaries in all the lands.
So the planks divide
and a salt blood covers you in life
as you go down? Rescue is only wind at play
on the long prairies of water.
Your choice is to believe it and drown,
or to drown, simply.

II
SEA CHANGE

But slowly twilight gathered up the skiffs
Into its long gray arms; and though the sea
Grew kind as possible to wrack-splayed birds;
And though the sea like woman vaguely wept;
She could not hide her clear enduring face,
Her cold divinities of death and change.

James Wright

BEYOND THE DREAM HATCH

A blind lash of hemlock
turns from the wind. The dock
sways, treble and negative photo image
in the tin calling
of crows. I hear drowned seamen
of *The Dragon's Wish* caressing
St. Bridget's wrist under muck
and sunken blankets of jetsam.
One song for them. One
for the mill-ends bobbing
in a great cold plate
of foam. What they say is
change
can bring you here.

THE DREAMS OF CELLOS

Why? A lion in underwater
        sunlight
suggests an angel, the slumbering
future of God. Heisenberg's
        uncertainty
rises like a mist toward the compulsion
to speak, the absolute necessity
        for silence.
A special roaring cast up
like a shoe on the beach means *penny*
or *exist* or *the shocked music*
        of pearls.
Blue now, thoughtful
as the tides clutch
our heap of stones, the lion signals
for more light,
        a deeper
sense of the wreck to come.
He is so quiet as he does this
he might be dying
        of happiness
or the dreams of cellos.

CINNAMON IS THE SECRET

Cinnamon is the secret
she said, stirring the chowder,
very quiet and without sadness.
You have to add it slow
like rock chipping away in a slow
stream, like a woman
sleepwalking through pain
in a story. And it must be
like a story
told purely, remorseless
as that ending
you spend your life trying
to change, that ragged lack
of a scar where the last spice
dissolves.

THE PITCHER'S PRIDE

At sixteen I wanted only
the hard laced scars
of dead horse
blurring from my fingers
as the batter winced
and rode forward
into failure. All dreaming
was a pistol shot,
the ball exploding
in the catcher's glove;
the ump's right arm flying
up, recording the kill.
On my little tower
of earth I was close
enough to God:
I could see my sin
dissolving in thunderclaps
of His applause. *Atta way
to fire, my son.*
When the arm went
years later
in rainy McMinnville
I had prayed forgive
please thy humble servant
his power to mow 'em down
to bleached fear and the dull
lives calling slowly in
across the trimmed outfield
turned brown.
I paid for that
by wanting,
every day always
through the ice packs
and cortisone
and my own brown grass, wanting
forever
one more game.

CHANCE

I shouted warning, cursed as the square teeth broke
that life and let the feathers spin a slow rain
through the rest of the day and into the dark.
It only meant to make a low pass

> *Out of control, bullets slice through the crowd.*
> *The arrow falls precisely inaccurate*
> *on the wrong deer (another fawn claws its severed spine*
> *into the same sumac brake).*

by the barn.
But, like a gate slamming, the mare lifted her head
above the slat fence and into the piercing chord of that
old suitor of a chance misstep, old red claw, weasel

> *Orders come, "Exercise maximum force*
> *ratio in sector 'B,' unfriendly," and are misunderstood*
> *by Lt. Calley, by a prehensile nightmare of triggers and pins*
> *and flight.*

rattling the stargate of an infant's sleep.
What bird could have known a horse would bite
through the probable order in less time
than life takes

> *Smoke hangs 20 years above rice paddies*
> *abandoned by the birds. Cornfields shrink imperceptibly.*
> *The next ice age uncoils its colder*
> *and colder dream.*

to fly away.
Yes, this is about a bird eaten by the brown mare. Sunlight
flutes on the muddied feathers. Crows pick the small head
clean.

SPIRIT HOVERING ABOVE THE BOX FLAG-DRAPED

The day is dry,
not like he remembers, not
as blue. Years under jungle
and the scarlet crown of war
have blurred even the edges of peaks
looming in the west.
He desires magpies,
jet and white breast-stroking
the belled light through cottonwoods;
but the sky will not produce them.
Among women he floats, obscure
canoe of memory and air.
Where is the green glove
by which the torn world is repaired?
With last year's leaves,
he scarcely knows. Friends,
the land, his wife and sons — all
let him fade *God rest his soul.*
So far from here, so quick
the fire went out.
There was no chance
for anything but death.
And here it is
again, this time for show
or for whatever
lets the living turn away and spit
and say *poor bastard; goodbye;*
and *welcome home.*

LIBERTY & TEN YEARS OF RETURN
—for the veterans

I

In the singed breath of London
we were lost
and aching sailors burnt by ships.
Disgusted, lonely, broke we four
buddies went adrift, sealed
casks of withered lust. Above the dim
lamps our President kept saying, "No.
We love a rigid chaos. Get laid
if you like, but nobody leaves."

II

A few cops passed like blue
trees moving. A taxi splashed dark
on our dark American frowns.
Hours we spoke of the trains, chanting,
mythical; of penalties
for missing muster, ship's movement,
the long glide home. At last, shivering
we stared down years of open windows
till the third-class cars pulled out
for Portsmouth in the teeth of dawn.

III

None of us expected this
arrival, the band strewn dead
on an empty pier, the fleet crusted
and opening like a bowl of dazed peonies
to the chalk sky. Now
we see: ours is an absent life, no healing.
Sent over the great sea
a decade has returned us with no riches,
no message, and no home waiting
or wanting us here.

GREETING THE GHOSTLY ROSE
Memorial Day

The skull-plate blooms rose fire
above the year, 1953. Were I angel
I would touch grandfather's face
resting in those petals
as the John Deere snores among rows
of peach trees; would lift Donny Maust
and Bobby Stanley from the rivers
of drowned-at-play.

*

But on my corner the planet's dead stay
dead. Little rose that is flowering out
in flame, give me a word for growing
that does not tick. Here in my room
so close to the sleep of birds
I have wept and eaten a bread of mist
and care and the love of single moments.
A few jars of twilight spill from the wall
where each thing blossoms once
because that is its beautiful desire.
And in this light I will admit grief,
my friends, though I do not know
how to greet it or how to bring you
these flowers.

IN FOUR PARTS

Detritus　　　　　　*Jettison*　　　　　*Olive Branch*
Seizures of the dust whispered out
in dreamsweat.

Crematorium　　　　*Statuary*　　　*Revive Me Lord*
Bread lost at the back of the skull, hysteria of sacred
rats discovering psychology under a mask of horn.

Loongrass　　　　　*Contagion*　　　　　　*The Face*
One human allotment: the given, what drifts
from the body as it sighs into the attitude which
has awaited it.

Grief　　　　　　*Whistle a Tune*　　　　　　*Grief*
For you, one kiss in three: the reverse of God:
the lifetime searching its sandstorm for a rose.

LIGHT, SUDDEN, BREAKS IN SHAFTS FROM HER

Her children sleep in their strangers' faces.
Her man is cloud and far away
and she is dancing. Thin. Even as blood
dissolving, she burns a liquid grace.
                                          This is
no accident. She'd planned for weeks
to strip and spin; letting the wrist curl
like beckoning, the thighs flash and part
and scissor into air.
                        It is a calm dis-
ease she wears, exotic as a picture floating
through the wall. It is as though
a swan longed to be
a swan.
            As though to that folding out
she, swirling, knows
no mate so fine as solitude
will ever bow
or enter.

NOTES

> *. . . the flames may burn the oboe*
> *but listen buddy boy they can't touch the notes!*
> — Galway Kinnell

Green bird the tree
of blues is just as high as you. Branches
in throat, lungs letting everything fly through and roots
in the heart: rhythmic pulsar also of tanager
and wren. No idea
bends too deep, too shyly in scarlet
reeds of the human. Outside my window
the tree is everything indigo coming in
flute and horn. To be satisfied is to misunderstand
your own rosetta; a ragged grackle of it bearing the everyday
cracked blue eggs under the mimosa.

Whatever sings will not desert its blood paling
in dense Spring, the bark and finches and pears.
How evening blossoms through its clarinet silver nerves of moonlight!
They who long to live keep listening. Those blue leaves
torn out of God return music for planet, the sublime
equation swaying, caught in its own arms or branches.

TWO FOR JAMES WRIGHT

I

News: he has darkened a boat
on the channels of salt unbelievable.
All gifts are dust to him now. Now memory
his only face choked with evening
and a few dreams. Breath is stunned out
of his verses, for a little while
they drift out from shore with him
as he starts across.

II

Come in from the fields, it is hot. Some angels
sleep by the pump. Go out
at dawn when the crows are white: no life
is wasted. Go out at noon
to the shaded hammock swinging
in a thick loss called wind. Bless the wheat
and the broken men who come over the hill.
History is the left hand dropping leaves in the river
of leaves and the river and the leaves.
What defeats us defeats us.

Out of pain and knowledge
of pain we are given the secret names
which love Earth, which stay, incredible
and tenuous on the cool tongue. Despair
is for gods. He was flesh and shine,
praise him. He was a notch in air
collecting dew and waving to the birds.
Praise. No reason completes itself.
Gone. No reason completes itself.

I will cup to my face
a dim time, the kindness there. Ashes
and loveliness. One shadow lies down
in the sun.

A REMINDER TO THE CURRENT PRESIDENT
—for Lewis Cook, 1945-1969

On an average afternoon men lay down
rifles, leaning into heat
from which a few will not rise
again. "It is because of shrapnel"
we say. "It is because of hatred
and ageless dispute and love
of country, which we have learned."
Though the cleanly young seem deathless
as this language passes over them,
neither the *zip* nor the sound of the plane
nor the singing wakes them.

On an average afternoon
by the trimmed shores, pacing, waiting
for news, the loved ones
approach the exact moment
which will not decode: a projector runs
on and on in a dark theater
and the doors are locked. A drumroll
circles the drillfield. Carbines
sound once, twice, and again. Who
will cast dirt down into the cool rest
of itself? Why does the film go on
showing and showing these few gathered
in sunlight around a space so empty
only the earth can fill it?

Questions. We are advised to let them ride.
We are advised that life continues.
That, on an average afternoon, the mother
will be given medals and a speech.
That all of this will be long ago,
like an unused wisdom.

"God's flag is our flag," it says
in the handbooks. "Therefore, be comforted
and clean of conscience: these deaths
are part of a plan." Meanwhile, the film
is rewinding; and the sound of a plane sails
the dimming heavens, far off, like a telegram
on its way.

THE TELL-TALE ANGEL

The neighborhood lamps are dark
bowls of sleep behind curtains. Overhead, burning
eyes of aircraft seek the shores
prepared for them.
                      The passengers look down into their lives
splashed with lights as though reflecting heaven.
High in the bright city a few night hawks cry and circle
an endless hunger.
                    The sort of night for angels, the sharp
quiet says; though who could bear to see them
playing their guitars, calling up the thick firmament
                                        to a god
sunk thousands of years in his dream? Would you kiss
an angel, your shreds of heart longing for daybreak like hosannahs
in the ruined hair of language?
                          Just once, imagine!
those silver lips. Those bells that never ring, they are so happy,
so unlike the world.

ON THE LAREDO LINE

Bread thrown from the last car
of evening. Moonlight.
Deep glow in the circle of angels
always watching. This land:
basalt knuckled hills. Mist
over the mountain
breathes like a red bird
changing to a cloud.
North, my old direction, let me love
something vast:
earth's dream-riddled face,
this night of one star
cleaving to the tracks.

THE DREAMER'S FUTURE

Mist in the alders touched
with grey. To wake here:
smell of fern and darkness: a drum
miles deep in magma miles deep
in loam. The beetle has ceased
pushing a star between galaxies
and now rests, covered with silver
and the stunned sighs of those
who looked suddenly up. A choir
of iron horses stands in shadow
waiting to begin.

ABOARD THE SAN JUAN FERRY

That we coast island to island
in our named lives
is nothing to bother earth's gleaming
blood. Above us, as the ferry swings
in toward shore, sea birds whirl
like bits of paper in the blue bowl
of the day. "We have come,"
we say. "We have made another
crossing, and the sea behind us
is entirely new."

III
SOTTO VOCE

Here on the edge of living, after rolling down my whole life like
 an instant, I look at myself.
Were you on this earth, love of my life? Will I ask myself this
 when at the end I know myself, when I recognize myself,
 and I awake,
newly risen from the earth, and I touch myself, and sitting in the
 ravine, at the end, I look at a sky shining with mercy?

Vincente Aleixandre

THREE DEATHS AND ANOTHER START

Out back where the orchard throws
ghosts of its apples down,
I sit shaded by leaves and what I always knew
sits by me,
        growing sharp.
If my bent grandfather sat here
knowing the exact pace at which life is undone,
he did not tell me.
If Bobby the boy who drowned
came like this to the suckhole of his spinning
out of light, he winged it off like a bruised windfall
                        sweetening the air.
So I tell myself I am the first man here
in a doomed face, seeing the trees go down
like the young go down in war. I am the first
last sayer of this time
in a small space that has done no harm, nor raised
a grandfather back to hold
                      the dozers in their muttering
place. And I can't stop them either. God knows
or ought to know how farms and small boys sink,
time heavy around their feet
and birdsong swimming the ignorant blue Cascade
Range lifting and falling off
both ends of history and prayer.
                            God knows
or ought to know I'm getting old and the dogfish
cleaned their teeth on Bobby's bones
now thirty years ago. And the farm slips
from my fingers while I watch shadows roll out
their graceful tangled art, and say goodbye.
It's time for another start.

ONE VISION

The plover alone in a field
in a flat pool of rain leans down
and his long beak breaks the membranous
dish, releasing dreams of earthworms,
the shadows of drowned grass.

This is a gift to me
because I have seen it
and the great mountain rising up behind it
and the fences that slouch against possession
framing it.

I wish I could say that I had never seen
such a thing before or since,
or that seeing it meant: "You have wasted
nothing. Forgive yourself."

FIRST SNOW

I wake in the hard
breath of my window
which, open all night, has admitted
some few small pages
of the first snow. October
is early for snow, and yet the old
remember the old
great storms searing out
of the aspen-littered hills
of September, falling like wolves
on the plain. There won't be
storms like that no more. There won't
be any real depth of white
except what piles up
on the head, hee hee, these
days. So
they speak, watching the sky, the ridges
of blanched air melting through
lemons and rust
in the upper branches.

*

This afternoon I make tea
and sit where the old fir nudges
at the glass and winter birds
lift their beaks, testing the day,
wondering is this their season
come round again
or at last.

IN GREY WATER: THE DAY

I

Slack tide before dawn.
The rental boats
have just finished singing.
A blue heron slivers, exact
glass at the grey edge
of grey water. Light aches
like a lover deep in the reeds,
in the pit of the willow shaking
with dark. Mussels, the violin
bones of flounder, all dead
given up by the nightly sea
arch in a tuning of instruments.
Memory and sun collide in the lungs
of stones and mud, breathing
the alchemical father, burning the skin
from his dream. The heron gives
his wing to the first shaft
of knowledge suddenly torching
its own face. For an instant,
which is the sea, and which
the bitter shore? Then morning lifts
its flat conch wail.

II

On thick glass the grebes
and sawbills move
like light finally
    broken
through waves of rain. I
    bend to that
mirror the starved
face of a reed. I ask, my
lips barely moving, for depth
    and power
and a sure, unselfish mind.
Clouds appear, sliding
like ghost-riders
into the southeast. The water
shakes from its trance,
    dissolving
the lives held there
and the supplications
which rise and are carried off
by the kingfisher
who has mistaken them
for the shimmer
of living things.

III

Barnacles and mussels
seem the heart
of the matter: there are so many
destroyed white faces clinking
and clinging to stones.
And they have voices like sticks
        snapping. All day
they argue cosmologies, relentless
as the salt which scrapes them
clean. It cannot be *the stars
are a wheel of winking
        pearl; all lands planets
in a universe of sea.* It cannot
be *God is a heron
from the far side of the cove.*
        Hours deepen
toward the minds of roses
far inland. Tide collects
for the long climb back
up the seawall, over moonwhite
        collars
of the dead. Over the heart
of the matter.

IV

Over water the twinkling
half-star windows of my country
come. Broken fences and battered
doors go with them. Voices
        of bruised
lives are nearly still. We have
        been surprised
by quiet and the warm rippling spears
of light on water, water on the face
of the mind. Discouragements
do not matter. Acrimony
        lies idle
licking its paws. What we know
is night and dark drifting with teal
far out in splashes of moon
and shadow. Tonight I am
        praying
again. I am praying the torn tongues
of Earth, the carborundum lament
of industrial sedge. What we keep
is what we allow no breaking of.
Membranous and steady, like wind
moving in the darkening neighborhoods,
we seek the far shore. And window light
breaks from us
like the sound of oars.

OR LAUGH

Having come to the glittering city,
having found the one leaf
on the one tree trembling,
having cast away stones and commenced
music, I offer you this the sweet pulp
my song.

*

O the adornments of her
where they lay scattered by passion!
O that passion God grant us all
one more time, at least,
in this life. See against the white
sheet her dancing slowly blossoms.
See the hand that writes in air
the lips' subtlest name
pressed to a mirror of flesh.
Rocking where the world touches praise,
mortal face to mortal face,
what could we do but sing out
of our clothes? Or laugh?

FLIGHTS THE WIRE BIRD WATCHES
—for Carlos

Low hills white, soft
humps in the waning day.
I am bound out
past saloons, whitewashed
former gas stations selling tacos,
fifteen farming equipment companies:
ragged edge of a county seat in the West.

Brown rouge clings
to the valley. Bright broken fists
of the Cascades lurch up
from cloud-choked distances.
A wire bird in a cornfield
breaks thinly into song.
What I wanted was not here.
Where I'm going the wire bird knows.
See, how joyous his singing,
how clear, among the crows.

AT THE EQUINOX

I

It is after the rain
and before the rain
and the smell is a smell of soil
drinking and sighing.
Dogs play with the vacancy
of the vacant lot across the street.
Birds are dipping very fast
very suspiciously;
in the gun blue air
all of them are black.

I can hear a tree nearby
beginning to hum out a little Mozart,
beginning to break the vows of silence
trees take, beginning (what the hell,
it's Spring) to let go
of her impossible strength.

The new shower falls
or rises from the ground
and a short avalanche of birdsong,
like a cheer, rushes from all directions
to nest in the branches
of the non-conformist.

II

Now day is nearly gone.
My white cat is the only cat
in sight. He crosses the road
to leave his scent on some bus tires.
Softly he calls to one of his brotherhood
hidden in the darkness. Then
he comes back
and watches the white rose
draw night slowly down
around its shoulders.

THE DEATH OF GIOVINE

Giovine went out among the darkling
up-sprayed winter trees, when the snow came
soft through an eternity of sky
as though the earth were calling back
fragments of its angels
who had gone off somwhere and stopped singing.

Giovine went out among a deepening bright
reflection and had no fear at all.
Smoking and walking and losing his way,
he yet thought, "This is a fine grove, and this.
See, though I am lost, the blessings rise up
around me." Thus he spoke, old Giovine,
loveliest of wordmakers, good king of stones
who carried no stones, who walked
for the love of walking
when he could have flown.

And then he sat down to rest
under the resting hemlocks, the cold
hemlocks that later called and called
to wake Giovine who had gone off—like the angels—
walking and singing in the other world
while his body sat as though thinking
of good friends and wine and a morning
fairer than this one, fairer than any
morning that has ever been.

GESTURE TO THE CAGED CRICKET

No depth of cawing
in the snowed railyards
measures the heart
given compulsively. Though
I wrap my hands in cloth
and bow to you, your silly blood
tap dances to a flat sky
painted last week by the butcher's son
who spied and caught you. So much
brown grass is quiet now
and I drink a green one-note
burning dusk's longest candle down
to no regrets. Who cares
for us together or apart
is one question answered by a song.
And who cares for song but singers
and the listener struck in white
blue shafts of night
by a window. It is late September
and he sings softly back to you.

KEEPING WATCH UNDER A LAMP POST IN THE DEEP WOOD I EXPERIENCE THE CARESS OF ANOTHER WORLD

So you have come at last,
my portion, circle
of light on the edge of the hill
of dark. I thought
you would be longer, narrowing down
from sun the pool of yourself
hung above me in the beeches.
                                      I thought
I would look out from your hand into stillness
puzzling the snow like footprints of a god.
But here you are, iced cyclamen
shuddering with wind. No women
follow you through the ruin of trees,
no friends at all heft axes over the fields
ritually asleep. It's just two
                            of us
trying to stay warm,
trying to say old roots twine in the deep
earth places, brother,
sister, keeper of what lasts
from one hill to the next.
We know it isn't love
buys this small space against the owls
                                    of blood
speaking their nameless question.
Still, midnight finds us kissing
just the same. Unknown lover
this kingdom of sticks
my life
burns like a black barn yearning for a heart.
The face of you worshipping no cup or stone
is not a fool's craving.
                      All right,
I mind my tongue
and keep my absent windows clear of God,

waiting like all desolate stars
for the light that never comes from you,
for the novas of the grass.

WHAT WAS A THIN WIRE

What was a thin wire
slowly turns thick and musical
in a sunlight unsuspected.
It is a wire of faith in something
or in nothing but itself.
Stretched out painfully year beyond year
over downed fruit and leaves
of the aging heart, the man
whose wire it was
could only think, "It
comes to nothing in the end
and before the end.
How shall I guard it as it disappears?"

What shall he say now
in the dawn with its blossoms
and oboes and all the birds come home
to the good trees?
He will say, "Be with me,
my own life, more precious to me
than the thin edge of the world
or the thin face
of what you do not have."

This is true. That man's days
were returned to him; and what he loved
reached out and touched him as though nothing
could touch him softly enough.